New Library of Pastoral Care
GENERAL EDITOR: DEREK BLOWS

Derek Blows is the Director of the Westminster Pastoral
Foundation and a psychotherapist at University College
Hospital. He is also an honorary canon of Southwark
Cathedral.

Family Matters

Titles in this series include:

Still Small Voice: An Introduction to Counselling
MICHAEL JACOBS

Letting Go: Caring for the Dying and Bereaved
PETER SPECK AND IAN AINSWORTH-SMITH

Living Alone: The Inward Journey to Fellowship
MARTIN ISRAEL

Invisible Barriers: Pastoral Care with Physically Disabled People
JESSIE VAN DONGEN-GARRAD

Learning to Care: Christian Reflection on Pastoral Practice
MICHAEL H. TAYLOR

Make or Break: An Introduction to Marriage Counselling
JACK DOMINIAN

Meaning in Madness: The Pastor and the Mentally Ill
JOHN FOSKETT

Paid to Care?: The Limits of Professionalism in Pastoral Care
ALASTAIR V. CAMPBELL

Swift to Hear: Facilitating Skills in Listening and Responding
MICHAEL JACOBS

Brief Encounters: Pastoral Ministry through the Occasional Offices
WESLEY CARR

Love the Stranger: Ministry in Multi-Faith Areas
ROGER HOOKER AND CHRISTOPHER LAMB

Being There: Pastoral Care in Time of Illness
PETER SPECK

Going Somewhere: People with Mental Handicaps and their Pastoral Care
SHEILA HOLLINS AND MARGARET GRIMER

Made in Heaven?: Ministry with Those Intending Marriage
PETER CHAMBERS

Helping the Helpers: Supervision and Pastoral Care
JOHN FOSKETT AND DAVID LYALL

A Dictionary of Pastoral Care
edited by ALASTAIR V. CAMPBELL